This book belongs to:

____

Made in the USA
Coppell, TX
31 July 2020

32201901R00066